To: The Music's

HENDERSON BEACH RESORT

We Enjoyed Hosting

You at Cuvee Bistro...

Happy Thanksgiving 2012!

Chef Greener

HENDERSON PARK INN

Exceptional Taste

Tales & Recipes

HENDERSON PARK INN

Exceptional Taste
Tales & Recipes

HENDERSON PARK INN

Exceptional Taste
Tales & Recipes

Published by Dunavant Gulf, LLC
Copyright © 2010 by Dunavant Gulf, LLC
3797 New Getwell Road
Memphis, Tennessee 38118

Executive Editor: William Hagerman, Managing Member/Senior Vice President, of Real Estate Operations
Managing Editor: Shannon Howell, President, DevCon Services Group, LLC

Jacket photography © by Henderson Park Inn
Pages 31 (small inset), 117, and 128 photography © by
 Art Morrison
Page 1 and 8 photography © by Bill Abbott
Pages 20, 21, 22, 23, 44, 45, 46, 47, 48, 49, 58, 59, 60,
 61 photography © by Arturos Studios
Pages 2, 3, 10, 11, 12, 13, 14, 15, 38, 39, 52, 53, 76–77,
 78–79, and 95 photography courtesy of
 Henderson Park Inn
Pages 30, 31, and 116 photography © by Michael Jay
Page 126 photography © by Michael Scott
Pages 4–5, 6–7, 8–9, 68–69, 94, 140–141, 156, 157,
 158–159, 160 photography © by Jason Chilton
Pages 146, 147, 148, and 149 photography © by
 Urban Design Associates
Food photography and page 84 © by Michael K Photography
Page 85 (small inset) photography © by Pure 7 Studios/
 Erica Manthey, owner

Food Styling by Jason Gouker and Tim Creehan
Recipes except as otherwise noted by Chef Tim Creehan
Pages 22–23 and 50–61 based on stories from Arturos Studios

Special thanks
Chef Alawna Middleton (page 33), Chef Charles Lee,
 Chef Greg Dupas, Chef Michael Rahmes, and
 Chef Jason Gouker
Destin Fishing Museum
Toni Ouellette
Brenda Barbee

Library of Congress Control Number: 2010 926 905
ISBN: 978-0-615-36276-2

Edited, Designed, and Produced by

FRP®.INC

a wholly owned subsidiary of Southwestern/
Great American, Inc.
P. O. Box 305142
Nashville, Tennessee 37230
1-800-358-0560

Editorial Director: Mary Cummings
Art Direction and Book Design: Starletta Polster
Project Manager: Cathy Ropp

Manufactured in the United States of America
First Printing: 2010
6,000 copies

To order Chef's Grill Plus® Instant Marinade, visit www.chefsgrillplus.com.

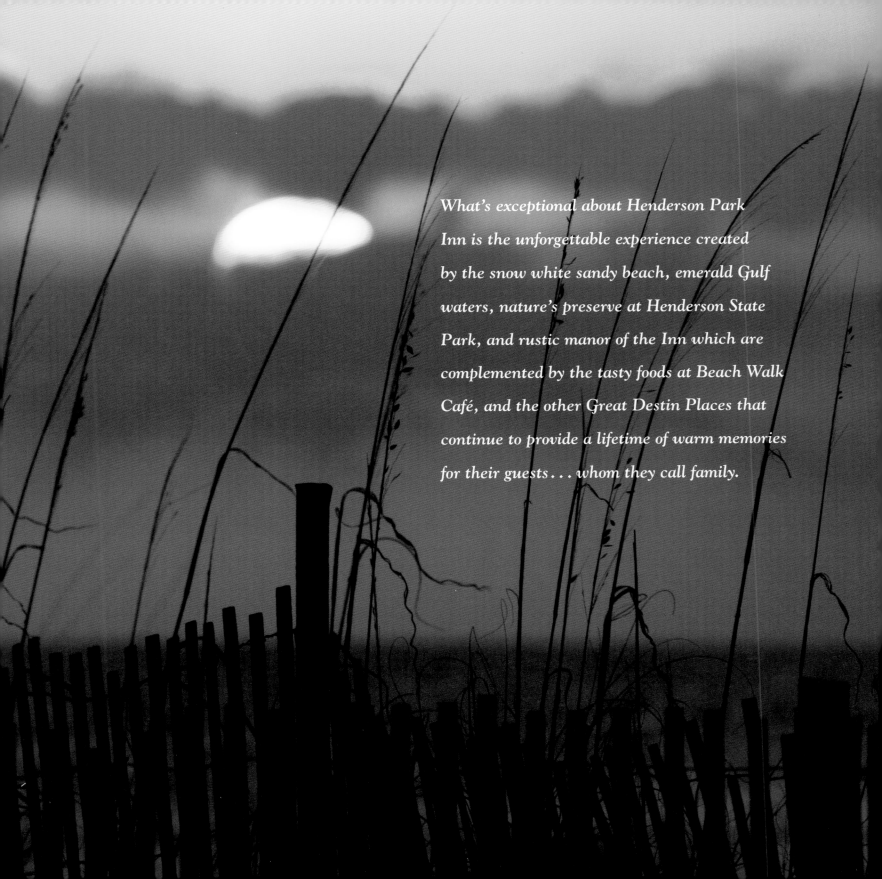

What's exceptional about Henderson Park
Inn is the unforgettable experience created
by the snow white sandy beach, emerald Gulf
waters, nature's preserve at Henderson State
Park, and rustic manor of the Inn which are
complemented by the tasty foods at Beach Walk
Café, and the other Great Destin Places that
continue to provide a lifetime of warm memories
for their guests . . . whom they call family.

Exceptional Contents

Exceptional Inn

Destin's Henderson Park Inn, locally known as simply The Henderson, has graced the northwest panhandle of Florida for some time. Bill and Steve Abbott, long-time Destin residents, were the original creators who, having grown up in Maine, were especially fond of their New England heritage.

Bill recalls that the "idea for the Inn was conceived from an old hotel where my father and I bell-hopped long ago—the Sparhawk Hotel in Ogunquit, Maine. The Sparhawk was a grand, old shingled hotel on the Atlantic Ocean and was owned by my uncle, Walter Abbott."

"The Sparhawk Hotel was one where guests often came for the entire summer. Most guests were from Boston and New York, who stayed in the same rooms year after year, came on Memorial Day, and left on Labor Day. There were porches, ballrooms, huge dining rooms, and tea parlors, all adorned with oriental carpets and beautiful wood walls. Breakfast and lunch were provided along with afternoon tea. No service was spared for the guests."

Bill fashioned the Henderson Park Inn from memories of his uncle's inn. The weathered and graying cedar shakes enveloping the two buildings at The Henderson continue, like the Sparhawk, to protect the Inn and its guests from nature's wrath and the erosion of time. The stately grays of the shakes reflect a New England flair coupled with the serenity of deep southern charm.

Today, no service is spared for our guests who, like those Bill remembers at the Sparhawk, are "some of the nicest folks in the world."

Exceptional Taste
Tales & Recipes

Ex·cep·tion·al

extraordinary; rare; superior; a common word the
guests use at the Henderson Park Inn.

Exceptional Taste is inspired by the many guests

of the Henderson Park Inn Bed-and-Breakfast who return again

and again to experience the *exceptional hospitality,*

exceptional views, exceptional food,

and an *exceptional piece of paradise.*

We find the *exceptional history* of the Inn, the City of Destin, and the many guests who frequent the Inn to be the root of this very unique location, which we believe to be the prettiest part of Florida. Tales of the early days of the City of Destin and the Inn are scattered throughout to provide glimpses of the unique atmosphere at the Henderson Park Inn.

Tastes of *exceptional culinary delights* from the private collection of Celebrity Chef Tim Creehan, reared from the depths of Louisiana and delicately seasoned by his training in New Orleans, are peppered among the pages of the book.

With this book, we have attempted to share a little piece of this *exceptional place* with you to take home and enjoy with your family and friends, while you daydream of your next visit to The Henderson Park Inn Bed-and-Breakfast in sunny Destin, Florida.

William O. Hagerman

William Hagerman
Senior Vice President of Real Estate Operations
Dunavant Enterprises, Inc. (current owner of the Henderson Park Inn)

Exceptional places are not created and sustained without *exceptional people*. Henderson Park Inn has had a wide array of these, including our owners, staff, associates, and, most important, guests.

Exceptional owners are few. They include the original developers, Bill and Steve Abbott, and current owners, Dunavant Enterprises. Building on the vision for the Henderson Park Inn begun by the Abbotts, William Hagerman, Senior Vice President from the Dunavant companies, had the vision of the property as one of the exceptional Signature properties for the Dunavant family.

Exceptional staff have been—and continue to be—the heart of the Inn since its very first day. Memories of pre-storm Henderson Park Inn were created by many of these special people. Some we recall are Susie Langford, Tamee Gaddis, Rudy Soliz, and Jim Olin. Post-storm, some of the same folks continue to make the Inn an exceptional place. Tamee Gaddis continues as Front Desk Manager. Rudy Soliz assisted greatly in reopening the Inn and then passed the torch as Chief of Maintenance to his nephew, Jeremy Soliz. Ryan Olin, Innkeeper since

ACKNOWLEDGMENTS

the post-storm reopening took place, was preceded by his father, Jim Olin, pre-storm CEO of the Abbotts. Newcomers who have made a place in the memories of many guests with their exceptional service include Laura, Rowie, and Renee.

Exceptional associates in business are especially important, and our exceptional ones have contributed much with their valuable skills and services. Among these are Beach Walk Café at Henderson Park Inn, with its fabulous and very talented culinary providers including founding Chef Tim Creehan, Chef Jason, Chef Mike, Breakfast Manager Marah Baltzell, and Marybeth Creehan, with other staff support Matthew, Nathan, Trevor, and Jim.

Exceptional guests—without whom the Inn would not be possible— we offer you a very special thank-you and acknowledgment.

Special thanks to photographers Michael K., Jason Chilton, and Art Morrison.

Special thanks to the contributing critics Beth Soucy, Alice Suttle, and Patrice Hagerman.

Breakfast ON THE Beach

French Toast

Cinnamon Rolls

Breakfast Potatoes with Onions
and Sweet Peppers

Fingerling Potato and
Sausage Hash

Chef Jason's Christmas-Morning Italian Strata

Quiche Base

Mushroom Fritta

Chef Alawna's Frittata

Cinnamon Roll French Toast

Pancake and Waffle Batter

Exceptional Taste

French Toast

SERVING SIZE: 4

5 each eggs – beaten
1 teaspoon vanilla extract
1¹/₂ teaspoons cinnamon
3 tablespoons sugar
¹/₂ cup milk
4 slices white or wheat bread – cut ¹/₂ inch thick
¹/₂ stick butter – melted

In a large bowl, blend the egg, vanilla, cinnamon, sugar and milk well.

Dip the bread into the egg mixture, coating both sides well. Set aside.

In a large nonstick sauté pan, heat the butter on medium heat. Place the toast in the pan and brown well; flip and brown the other side and remove. Cut on a diagonal and serve immediately dusted with confectioners' sugar to taste.

CINNAMON ROLLS

SERVING SIZE: 32

1	package frozen dinner roll dough	2	tablespoons cinnamon
1	cup raisins	1	box powdered sugar
2	sticks melted butter	1	cup milk
2	cups brown sugar		

Make the same as dinner rolls only knead raisins into dough.

After first rise punch down.

Turn out on a lightly floured board.

Roll out to 1/4 inch thick or less.

Brush one side with melted butter.

Sprinkle with brown sugar and cinnamon; roll up jelly roll style.

Cut into 1-inch slices and place on greased cookie sheet.

Let rise until double, almost 1 hour.

Bake at 375 degrees for 12 to 15 minutes.

GLAZE
Mix 1 box powdered sugar and enough milk to make thin enough to drizzle over rolls.

Deep Blue

The bountiful catch from the local waters was the foundation of the early settlement of the Destin area. The fishing industry sustained its growth and its eventual development as the most beautiful resort area on the Gulf coast.

Founding fishermen in the early 1800s used seine nets to catch fish near the shoreline. Eventually, these local fishermen began to venture further out into the deeper waters of the Gulf for a wider variety of species.

Photo by Arturo's Studio

Photo by Arturo's Studio

Exceptional Fishing

A feature called the 100 Fathom Curve is closer to the shoreline of Destin than at any other place along the Florida coast. This deep water is the beginning of the underwater canyon, Desoto Canyon, which at 3,000 feet deep is over half as deep as the Grand Canyon. Fishermen can reach these seemingly bottomless cobalt waters quickly, where hundred-pound sailfish and nine-hundred-pound blue marlin swim.

Anglers from all over the world come here to enjoy fishing in these Deep Blue Waters.

The East Pass—Aerial view, 1940s

The East Pass

The biggest engineering project completed in the area this century was accomplished by five fishermen armed only with a boat oar.

To enter the Gulf in the 1920s, you would go to the east end of the harbor, where Sand Piper Cove is located, to enter the East Pass Channel. It opened into the Gulf near where Pelican Beach Resort is located today.

There had been a tremendous amount of rain in 1926, and the Choctawhatchee River and Bay were at flood stage. The bay had risen about four feet higher than the Gulf, and the then restricted East Pass was not adequate to allow the rush of water to flow out. Every dock and many home sites were endangered.

Five hardy souls, Captain Dewey Destin Sr., Captain O.T. Melvin Sr., Dolph Weekly, Parker Owens, and Arn Strickland—armed with an oar from a skiff—made a small trench. A little trickle of water started going south into the Gulf. Within an hour there was a gully over a hundred feet wide. By the next morning, the "gully" was over a hundred yards across, and a new East Pass was formed.

Until then there had never been any money—not a dime—spent to maintain a channel in the Old Pass. It maintained an eight-foot depth and was a little more than one hundred feet wide. With the new pass letting more water out of the Choctawhatchee Bay than the Old Pass, it only took a few years before the Old Pass closed. The Corp of Engineers sent a dredge to straighten and make the new pass deeper and better. In the seventy-five years since it was started by a small group of men, there is no telling how much money has been spent to maintain what they built with nothing but an oar and muscle.

O. T. Melvin

Breakfast Potatoes with Onions and Sweet Peppers

Serving Size: 4

2	Idaho potatoes, large – peeled and cubed	1/2	gold bell pepper – cubed
1/4	stick butter	1/2	red and/or green sweet pepper – cubed
1	tablespoon canola oil	1/2	teaspoon garlic – chopped fine
1/2	yellow onion – cubed	to taste	black pepper
		to taste	salt

In a pot, cover the potatoes with water; bring to a slow boil.

Cook the potatoes till tender but not falling apart; drain and set aside.

Heat the butter and canola in a large sauté pan. Add the onions and sauté till starting to brown.

Add the sweet peppers, garlic and potatoes and lightly brown the potatoes.

Season to taste and cook until desired consistency. Serve immediately.

Fingerling Potato and Sausage Hash

Serving Size: 8

1 1/2 pounds fingerling potatoes – halved
1/4 cup olive oil
1/2 pound andouille sausage – cut 1/2 inch thick
1 yellow onion – diced
to taste kosher salt
to taste fresh ground black pepper

Preheat an oven to 375 degrees.

Toss all the ingredients together in a large mixing bowl, coating well and seasoning to taste.

Place this mixture in a large casserole dish or roasting pan. Bake in the oven for 35 minutes or until the potatoes are tender, stirring occasionally.

Serve immediately.

Chef Jason's Christmas-Morning Italian Strata

Serves 12

1¹/2	pounds sausage	2	teaspoons Italian seasoning
1	(12-ounce) loaf French bread	¹/2	teaspoon garlic powder
1	(8-ounce) can sliced mushrooms, drained	¹/4	teaspoon pepper
		2	cups mozzarella cheese, shredded
6	large eggs	1	cup Cheddar cheese, shredded
4	cups milk		

Night before serving:
Grease 13- × 9-inch glass baking dish. Crumble and cook sausage; drain. Cut bread into ¹/2-inch cubes. Combine sausage, bread and mushrooms and fill baking dish. Whisk together eggs, milk and spices; pour over bread mixture, being sure to evenly distribute liquid. Refrigerate, covered, for at least 8 hours.

Following morning:
Preheat oven to 350 degrees.

Bake strata for 1 hour, uncovered. Remove strata and sprinkle with cheeses. Bake an additional 15 minutes or until inserted knife comes out clean.

Let stand 10 minutes before serving.

 Quiche Base

Serving Size: 6

2 cups flour, all-purpose or wheat	1 1/2 cups Swiss cheese – grated
1/2 teaspoon salt	2 cups assorted vegetables, meats
3/4 cup vegetable shortening	or seafood
3 tablespoons water	1/4 cup Parmesan cheese – grated
4 eggs	to taste fresh ground black pepper
1/2 cup heavy cream	

Preheat an oven to 350 degrees. Soften the shortening and cut into the flour and salt with a pastry mixer or a potato masher.

Add the water 1 tablespoon at a time until a ball forms. In a 10-inch tart shell pan 2 inches deep, press the dough into the form and up the sides, making sure the bottom is thin and even. Prick the bottom with a fork.

Place the crust in the preheated oven for 10 minutes; remove and set aside.

Mix the eggs with the cream; add the Swiss cheese. Pour this mixture into the cooled crust. Add the selected ingredients and arrange in an attractive pattern.

Top this prepared quiche with the Parmesan cheese and black pepper. Bake for 25 to 30 minutes or until the center is firm. Remove and let stand for 20 minutes, cut and serve immediately or refrigerate for up to 2 days and reheat later.

Mushroom Fritta

Serving Size: 4

2 cups assorted fresh mushrooms
1/2 cup water
1 tablespoon fresh rosemary –
chopped fine
to taste kosher salt

to taste ground black pepper
2 cups rice flour
to taste white truffle oil
to taste Romano cheese – grated

Heat a gallon of canola oil to 350 degrees.

De-stem and break apart the cleaned mushrooms into bite-size pieces.

Place the water, rosemary, salt and pepper in a mixing bowl and blend.

Place the mushrooms in the water and coat.

Dredge the mushrooms in the flour and knock off any excess.

Drop into the oil and fry until brown and crispy; remove and drain.

Season with salt, pepper, truffle oil and cheese.

Serve immediately.

Chef Alawna's Frittata

SERVING SIZE: 1

Veggies of your choice
2   eggs
1/4   cup cream or half-and-half
1   teaspoon cheese blend

Sauté veggies, eggs, cream and cheese blend in an ovenproof skillet to a soft scramble.

Place in oven and bake at 450 degrees for 5 to 7 minutes.

Cinnamon Roll French Toast

Serving Size: 6 to 8

6   eggs
2   cups milk
1/2   cup sugar
1   tablespoon cinnamon
1   tablespoon nutmeg
1   teaspoon pure vanilla extract
Baked cinnamon rolls, sliced

Beat first six ingredients together. Dip each cinnamon roll slice into the batter.

Cook in a skillet over medium heat for 1 1/2 minutes on each side.

Top with confectioners' sugar and toppings of choice.

*NOTE: Use our recipe for Cinnamon Rolls (page 19)
or your favorite cinnamon roll recipe.*

Pancake and Waffle Batter

Serving Size: 6

2 1/4 cups all-purpose flour
3   tablespoons sugar
1   tablespoon dry yeast
1   teaspoon salt
1 3/4 cups warm milk (105 degrees)
1/4 cup butter – melted
1   each egg

Blend the flour with the sugar, yeast and salt.

Stir in the warm milk, butter and egg. Cover and let stand in a warm place till batter doubles in size.

Cook or refrigerate overnight.

Serve prepared pancakes or waffles with desired toppings such as confectioners' sugar, strawberries, maple syrup and/or butter.

Beachside Picnics

Gazpacho

Barbequed Chicken Chopped Salad

Chicken Salad

Pulled Pork Open-Faced Low-Carb Sandwich

Exploded Beef Spring Roll Salad

Chopped Beef Salad Wrap

Maque Choux Pasta Salad

Mediterranean Pasta Salad

Toasted Sesame Green Bean Salad

Mediterranean Green Bean Salad

Potato Salad

Beach Walk Cookies

Exceptional Taste

Gazpacho

Serving Size: 3

1/2 (28-ounce) can plum tomatoes, peeled with juice
1/2 medium yellow onion – peeled
1/2 small green bell pepper
1 clove garlic – peeled
1 tablespoon rice vinegar
1/2 lemon – juiced
1 teaspoon extra-virgin olive oil
1/2 jalapeno – cleaned
1/2 (11-ounce) can V-8 juice
2 tablespoons cilantro – chopped
to taste salt
to taste black pepper
as needed water
1/2 cucumber – diced
2 tablespoons red or gold pepper – diced

In a food processor, purée the first 10 ingredients well; chill for 30 minutes.

Season to taste, adjust consistency with water and serve garnished with the cucumber and peppers.

Serve chilled.

Barbequed Chicken Chopped Salad

Serving Size: 4

2 (6- to 8-ounce) skinless boneless chicken breasts
4 tablespoons Mesquite Grill Flavor Chef's Grill Plus® Instant Marinade
1 cup barbeque sauce (your favorite)
¼ cup sour cream
as needed water

1 head romaine lettuce – chopped and washed
1 vine-ripe tomato – diced
1 ear of corn – cooked, cooled and cut off the cob
1/2 cup black beans – cooked and drained
1/2 cup jicama – peeled and diced

Preheat a grill surface on high.

Brush the chicken with the Grill Plus® and cook until 145 degrees internal temperature. Baste with barbeque sauce and remove to cool to room temperature.

Blend the remaining barbeque sauce with the sour cream and water to achieve the desired dressing consistency.

Toss the romaine, diced tomato, corn, black beans and jicama and refrigerate.

Dice the chicken and toss with the prepared dressing and the salad mixture.

Serve immediately.

SERVING IDEAS: Can place the chicken on top of the salad mixture and serve the dressing on the side for a family-style presentation that will hold longer. Garnish with julienned strips of fried corn tortillas to make a Mexican BBQ chicken salad or serve over a tostada.

CHICKEN SALAD

SERVING SIZE: 4 TO 6

1 rotisserie chicken –
meat pulled from carcass and coarsely chopped

1 cup mayonnaise –
more or less may be used depending on the size and
yield of the chicken

1/4 cup of Dijon mustard
1 tablespoon chopped garlic
1 small bunch of chopped scallions
1/4 cup of chopped parsley
1/2 cup of chopped cashews
1/2 cup of halved red grapes
to taste kosher salt and black pepper

Mix all ingredients together.

Chill before serving.

The Destin Fishing Rodeo

The city of Destin has a rich fishing heritage dating back as early as the 7th century AD. to Native American inhabitants who were drawn by the climate and abundant fishing of the area.

Photo by Arturo's Studio

Photo by Arturo's Studio

Exceptional Tales

Destin's immediate history can be traced to a master fisherman, Captain Leonard Destin from New London, Connecticut, who settled here around 1835. Destin pioneered the fishing industry in Destin, and he and his descendents have fished the area for decades. Today, the largest and most elaborately equipped fishing fleet in Florida docks at the Destin Harbor.

Every year, the charter fleet gears up for one of the longest running fishing tournaments known—The Destin Fishing Rodeo. Started in 1948 by a small group of fishermen, the tournament was intended to extend the summer fishing season for visitors, to help raise funds for the Destin Community Center, and to boost the seasonal income of the fishing industry and community.

Photo by Arturo's Studio

Photo by Arturo's Studio

Destin Fishing Rodeo sailfish

Photo by Arturo's Studio

According to Captain Howard Marler, one of the tournament's founders, the first fishing rodeo was started to bring people to Destin, but it needed tweaking. "The first week-long Rodeos turned out real well, but we just weren't thinking right or something, because we were having it at the wrong time of year. We had people in here in the summer, and we needed it when we didn't have anyone coming but still had a lot of fish to catch. So we . . . set it up for October, and it's been that way ever since."

Exceptional Tales

GULF QUEEN

Exceptional Rodeo

After over 60 years, the now 31-day tournament has more than 100 categories of competition for 35 species of fishing and $100,000 in prizes. Since its inception, the Rodeo has hosted over a million anglers who, by participating in one of Destin's oldest traditions, maintain ties to its earliest heritage and legacy.

Pulled Pork Open-Faced Low-Carb Sandwich

Serving Size: 4

2 each Hormel pork osso bucco or Boston butts
1 cup water
1 each domestic beer
1 each tomato
1/2 cup raisin juice concentrate (RJC)
1/2 each canned black beans – drained
1 each tomato – diced
1 each ear of corn – cooked and cut off the cob

1/2 cup feta cheese – crumbled
2 tablespoons cilantro – chopped
1 teaspoon salt
4 slices low-carb wheat bread – grilled
4 slices queso blanco cheese
2 each red bell peppers – split in half
4 each green onions – grilled
1/2 cup raisin juice concentrate (RJC) – reduced by half

Preheat an oven to 450 degrees. Place the Hormel pork osso bucco in a pan with the water, beer, whole tomato and a half cup of RJC. Cover with foil and bake for 30 minutes.

Combine the next six ingredients in a mixing bowl; let stand at room temperature.

Remove the pork from the oven and let cool for 15 to 20 minutes. Pull the pork meat off the shank and leave in the braising liquid.

Cut the grilled bread and queso blanco on diagonal making two pieces per plate. Top each piece of bread with 3 ounces of pulled pork and one slice of cheese.

Place the salsa in the pepper half and garnish the plate with grilled green onion and reduced RJC glaze.

Exploded Beef Spring Roll Salad

SERVING SIZE: 4

2 cups tenderloin, beef – cut into 2-inch strips
1/2 cup soy sauce
3/4 cup sweet Thai chili sauce
1 teaspoon black pepper – freshly ground

1/4 cup rice vinegar
2 teaspoons smooth peanut butter
4 cups napa cabbage – shredded
1/4 cup carrots – grated
1/4 cup green onions – chopped
1/4 cup bean thread noodles – fried

Marinate the steak in the soy, 1/4 cup of the chili sauce and pepper for 4 hours.

Blend the remaining chili sauce, rice vinegar and peanut butter in a mixing bowl and refrigerate.

Grill and slice thin or fry and slice thin the meat.

Toss the meat with the prepared dressing, cabbage, carrots and green onions. Place on plates and garnish with crispy noodles.

SERVING IDEAS: Substitute shrimp or chicken for beef. The proteins can be grilled or lightly battered in corn starch and fried.

Chopped Beef Salad Wrap

Serving Size: 4

1/4 cup blue cheese – crumbled
1/4 cup spreadable brie
1/4 cup mayonnaise
2 tablespoons Creole mustard
1 tablespoon parsley – chopped
1 tablespoon green onion – chopped
2 tablespoons prepared horseradish
14 ounces sirloin strip steak roasted medium-rare – chopped

2 tablespoons red onion – diced
1/2 cucumber – diced
1 tomato – diced
2 heads romaine lettuce – chopped
4 whole wheat wraps
2 Idaho potatoes – sliced, blanched, fried and salted
4 clusters champagne grapes
4 strawberries

In a mixing bowl, combine the blue cheese, spreadable brie, mayo, mustard, parsley, green onion and horseradish. Refrigerate.

In another bowl combine the beef, red onion, cucumber, tomato and romaine. Dress with the blue cheese remoulade. Mix well.

Divide this mixture into 4 equal parts and place in the center of the wraps. Roll and cut on a bias.

Place the prepared wrap on a plate and garnish with fried potato chips, grapes and a strawberry.

Maque Choux Pasta Salad

Serving Size: 6

1/2 stick unsalted butter
1 teaspoon garlic – chopped
1/2 stick celery – diced small
1/2 each red pepper – diced small
1/2 each yellow onion – diced small
1/2 cup green onions – chopped
4 each ears of corn – cooked and cut off cob
1/2 cup sour cream
1/4 pound penne pasta – cooked and drained
to taste salt
to taste black pepper

In a large sauté pan melt the butter and sauté the garlic, celery, pepper and onions until tender.

Add the corn and heat through. Add the sour cream and remove from the heat, stirring until smooth.

Add this mixture to the pasta and blend well. Refrigerate 30 minutes and season to taste.

Mediterranean Pasta Salad

Serves 10

1   pound ziti pasta, cooked and cooled
1   (10-ounce) jar of spanish olives, drained
1/4   cup basil, chopped
1/2   cup olive oil
1/4   cup balsamic vinegar
1/2   small red onion, diced
1   red bell pepper, julienned
1/2   cup banana peppers, chopped
1/2   seedless cucumber, sliced
1   pint grape tomatoes, halved
to taste kosher salt and black pepper
1   cup feta cheese, crumbled

Cook pasta al dente and let cool completely.

Pulse olives in a food processor until slightly smooth with a few chunks.

Toss the olive purée and the next 8 ingredients with the pasta and season with salt and pepper.

Crumble the feta cheese on top and serve.

Toasted Sesame Green Bean Salad

Serving Size: 4

1 pound fresh green beans – snapped
1 each carrot – peeled, thinly sliced
3 tablespoons canola oil
1 clove garlic – minced
2 tablespoons sesame seeds
2 tablespoons pancake syrup
2 teaspoons sugar
3 tablespoons soy sauce

2 tablespoons rice vinegar
2 drops sesame oil
2 tablespoons cashews – chopped
1/4 each red and gold bell peppers –
    julienned
to taste fresh ground black pepper
to taste kosher salt

Bring a pot of water to a rolling boil and blanch the beans and carrots to desired doneness. Drain and shock with ice water; drain well.

Heat the canola oil in a sauté pan and lightly brown the garlic and sesame seeds (This happens quickly, so don't overcook); set aside.

Add the syrup, sugar, soy, vinegar and sesame oil to the sesame seed mixture.

Toss the beans and carrots with the sesame mixture, cashews and peppers and season to taste; marinate at least 1 hour or overnight.

NOTE: Green beans may be substituted with haricots verts, Chinese long beans or snow peas.

Luckiest Fishing Village In The World

The Luckiest Fishing Village In The World became the official nickname for Destin on October 15, 1956. My son-in-law, Arturo, got word from the News Wire that Florida's then Governor Leroy Collins was passing through Destin en route to open the Pensacola State Fair.

A governor or state official had never participated in the Destin Rodeo, but locals were able to maneuver the governor's entourage to the fishing docks to pose for a few pictures. I was standing by with a newly commissioned trolling vessel, the *Miss Kathy*.

(continued)

Exceptional Tales

Exceptional Luck

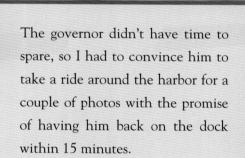

Photo by Arturo's Studio

The governor didn't have time to spare, so I had to convince him to take a ride around the harbor for a couple of photos with the promise of having him back on the dock within 15 minutes.

I set a few rods with line out to make it appear that the governor was fishing. While Arturo snapped promotional pictures, I made one pass around the sea buoy and was on the way back in, when who would get a strike but Governor Collins. It wouldn't happen again in a million years.

When Governor Collins arrived in Pensacola, all he talked about was his Destin fishing trip. Articles with pictures about his visit circulated throughout the South. One reporter questioned the governor: "That's hard to believe that you could head out and return to the dock with a 19-pound King Mackerel within 15 minutes."

The governor just smiled and replied, "Not if you're fishing out of Destin. Them boys live with the fish. Destin's the "World's Luckiest Fishing Village." The phrase became official . . . and Destin hasn't been the same since.

—*Reddin "Captain Salty" Brunson*

Governor Collins with 19-pound King Mackerel

Mediterranean Green Bean Salad

Serving Size: 6

3/4   pound baby or snap beans – blanched and chilled
1   cup grape tomatoes – split
1   cup roasted sweet peppers – chopped
1   recipe balsamic vinaigrette page 59 *The Simple Cuisine*
1   teaspoon garlic – chopped
to taste kosher salt
to taste fresh ground black pepper

Combine all the ingredients in a mixing bowl and toss; let stand 30 minutes or refrigerate overnight. Serve room temperature or chilled.

Potato Salad

Serving Size: 8

5 each medium to small potato – peeled
1 medium yellow onion – peeled
4 each radishes
2 each eggs – boiled and cooled
1 each rib celery – diced small
2 each green onions – chopped
2 tablespoons parsley – chopped

2 each garlic cloves – chopped
1/3 cup mayonnaise
1 teaspoon Dijon mustard
to taste salt
to taste white pepper
as needed water

Place the potatoes whole under water in a pot. Place on high heat and boil until almost cooked. Remove and cool.

In a mixing bowl, with a box grater, grate the yellow onion, radishes and egg.

Add the celery, green onion, parsley, garlic, mayonnaise and mustard; blend well. Set aside.

Cut the cooled potatoes into cubes and blend with the prepared mixture; season to taste and adjust consistency with water. Chill or serve immediately.

Beach Walk Cookies

SERVING SIZE: 4 DOZEN

1 cup soft butter
2/3 cup sugar
1 cup brown sugar
2 1/2 cups all-purpose flour
1 tablespoon baking soda
1 tablespoon salt
2 each eggs
2 cups filling

Cream butter, sugar and brown sugar together.

Sift remaining dry ingredients together; set aside.

Add eggs to butter and sugar one at the time.

Add dry ingredients slowly and mix until just combined.

Fold in filling. (Filling can be any dry ingredients such as chocolate chips, oatmeal, nuts, raisins, etc.)

Bake at 350 for 6 to 10 minutes.

La Fountain's Wharf

The first restaurant in Destin, La Fountain's Wharf, was started by Vernon "Bud" and Joyce La Fountain in May of 1960. Bud was stationed at Eglin Air Force Base across the bay from Destin, and when he was discharged he and his wife decided to settle in Destin, working some odd jobs. While on the docks one day, Coleman Destin suggested to Bud that he open a restaurant. Coleman leased a dock and built a small one-room restaurant. The most expensive thing on the menu was the seafood platter, which included fried fish, oysters, scallops, shrimp, and a deviled crab. It was served in a woven basket and cost $2.50. Later, they added a broiled version of the seafood platter. La Fountain's Wharf was in operation until Bud's death in 1988.

Sunset Toasts

Lemouroudji

Frozen Grasshopper

Espresso Martini

Rum Punch

Garlic Aïoli

Crab Meat Butter

Baked Brie with Apricot Glaze

Baja Fish Taco

Sun-Dried Tomato Bruschetta

Coconut Shrimp with
Jalapeno Dipping Sauce

Crispy Shrimp Crostini with
Marinara Sauce

Fried Plantains

She-Crab Soup

Lobster Bisque

Cheddar, Pancetta and Leek Soup

Roasted Tomato Soup

Exceptional Taste

*L*EMOUROUDJI

SERVING SIZE: 12

1   each lemon
2   each pieces ginger
to taste cayenne pepper
1   gallon water
1   cup sugar

Juice the lemon.

Peel and grate the ginger.

Place the grated ginger and a liberal dash of the cayenne pepper into a piece of cheesecloth and tie it into a knot.

Let soak in the water. After 15 minutes or so, add the sugar and the lemon juice. Chill and serve.

Frozen Grasshopper

Serving Size: 1

1   ounce green crème de menthe
1   ounce white crème de cacao
3/4   ounce cream
Ice

Using a blender filled with ice, combine all ingredients. Serve in a chilled cocktail glass.

*"Sugary white sand, mild sea breeze,
umbrella shade, cold drink…
remind me again as to what we were discussing."*

Espresso Martini

Serving Size: 1

1   serving brewed espresso
1   ounce Godiva chocolate liqueur
3/4   ounce Kamora coffee liqueur
3/4   ounce Stolichnaya vanilla vodka
3   coffee beans

Combine first 4 ingredients inside a shaker filled with ice. Shake vigorously to mix.

Strain into a martini glass and garnish with coffee beans.

Only Irish coffee provides in a
single glass all four essential food groups:
alcohol, caffeine, sugar, and fat.
—Alex Levine

Rum Punch

SERVING SIZE: 1

2   ounces Mount Gay rum
1   ounce pineapple juice
1   ounce guava juice
1   ounce fresh orange juice
1/4   teaspoon freshly ground nutmeg
1   cherry

Combine the first 4 ingredients inside a tall glass filled with ice. Mix well.

Garnish with a sprinkle of nutmeg and a cherry.

*"Sweet Tea, like life,
must be created by mixing ingredients while hot,
otherwise it is simply tea with sugar."*

Garlic Aïoli

SERVING SIZE: 8

1 cup garlic cloves
1 cup chicken stock
1 tablespoon olive oil
3/4 cup sour cream
to taste salt
to taste white pepper

Boil the garlic in the chicken stock until soft.

Remove from the stock, drain and sauté in the olive oil until browned.

Purée the garlic in a food processor with the sour cream until smooth and season to taste.

Serve chilled at room temperature as a sauce for vegetables or fish or in place of mayonnaise.

A Tale of Two Hurricanes

The eye of Hurricane Ivan came ashore at 3 a.m. on September 16, 2004, about 100 miles west of Destin at Gulf Shores, Alabama. At landfall, it was a Category 3 storm packing winds of 130 miles per hour. Residents who evacuated the area returned to find damage around town including fallen trees, roof damage, and damage to docks and piers as well as to boats. About 250 homes were uninhabitable by law until major repairs took place.

Exceptional Tales

There's Room at the Inn

"The light on the porch of the Henderson Park Inn beckons guests once again into the New England-style building previously intended for demolition," reported *Destin Daily News* writer Robbyn Brooks, in her October 2005 article.

It was a hurricane that closed the doors of the Inn and a hurricane that reopened them. After Hurricane Katrina, the damaged Inn was sitting idle while plans were in the process for a new Henderson Beach Resort. However, spurred by Lucy Kisela, wife of Destin City Manager Greg Kisela, Bill Hagerman, Senior VP for the new owner, Dunavant Enterprises, agreed to reopen the Inn for hurricane evacuees. It was a large undertaking and was a testament to the Destin Community and the caring attitude still exhibited from the early pioneers to today.

Coordinating carefully and diligently, Ms. Kisela brought together the city leaders with Dunavant Enterprises to ensure that the operation was supported. Both groups felt that a strong management company was needed to supervise the admission of evacuee guests. Immediately, Jeanie Daly, owner of Newman-Daly Resort Management, came to mind, and she graciously agreed to volunteer her services.

Hurricane Katrina batters Louisiana, Mississippi, and Alabama, sending carloads of evacuees to Destin as the area responds with generous donations and help.

Now, how to make this happen? Well, Ms. Kisela happened to be the Administrative Manager of Olson and Associates, whose owner, Rick Olson, had contacts that he used to get the basic repair work completed.

Now, how do you decide to whom to offer this service? Over 100,000 persons were displaced, and the Inn only has 35 rooms. The City tackled this task, interviewing hundreds of applicants to determine where the need was most suited. Families were ushered in and welcomed the Inn's homey atmosphere.

Now, how do we help care for these folks? The Village Baptist Church, the Inn's closet church neighbor, stepped forward to minister to these families. Each and every day, the Village congregation brought food and other needed supplies to the Inn, served the food, and was there to encourage the families through the crisis. Moms and dads with nowhere to turn had listening ears and helping hands; scared kids with an uncertain future had a place to call home; and the congregation was able to show God's love to every family during the stay at the Inn.

After many months, each family was able to start its recovery, and each eventually went home to start over, move to other areas, or even stay in Destin to become part of the community fabric they experienced while at the Inn.

Exceptional Hospitiality

CRAB MEAT BUTTER

SERVING SIZE: 12

2 sticks unsalted butter
8 ounces Philadelphia Cream Cheese – softened
1 cup sour cream
1 pound jumbo lump crab meat, pasteurized or fresh – shells removed
pinch of kosher salt
to taste cayenne
2 green onions – minced

Over a double boiler melt the butter with the cream cheese and sour cream.

Fold in the crab meat and warm through.

Season to taste and finish with the minced green onions.

*SERVING IDEAS: Great as a warm appetizer served in
individual pastry cups or on crackers. Alternatively, use as a topping for a
grilled steak, pork, veal or chicken breast.*

Baked Brie with Apricot Glaze

SERVING SIZE: 6

3 each small brie cheese wheels
4 ounces apricot jam
4 ounces sliced almonds – toasted
1 loaf tuscan bread – sliced $1/3$ inch thick
4 tablespoons olive oil
1 tablespoon garlic – chopped
2 tablespoons parsley – chopped

Warm the brie in the oven or microwave until just soft.

In a sauté pan warm the jam and add the almonds.

Brush the bread with the olive oil and garlic and grill lightly.

Serve the warm brie with the apricot glaze over the top and finish with the chopped parsley.

Baja Fish Taco

Serving Size: 4

1¹/₂ pounds fish
2 limes – juiced
1 garlic clove – chopped
2 tablespoons salad oil
1 teaspoon Maggi seasoning
to taste salt
to taste black pepper

Blend all the ingredients in a marinating pan and let stand 30 minutes.

Grill and serve immediately.

*NOTE: The marinated fish can be substituted with shrimp,
scallops and lobster. The traditional taco is served in a warm flour tortilla
with thin shaved cabbage and salsa.*

The marinade may be heated and served over the fish as a sauce.

*You can, however, serve the taco in a different shell and with
a wide variety of southwestern condiments.*

Exceptional Tales

Beach Front Proposal

I am not emailing to make a reservation. However, I am emailing about my experience at your restaurant. On March 19th, I asked my girlfriend to marry me at the Beach Walk Café. Specifically, this happened on the beach with the help of your Toes in the Sand dining opportunity. From the time I called to inquire about the possibility to eat dinner on the beach to the last bite of our Key lime pie; I was extremely pleased with the professionalism and quality of your staff. Although I think she would have said yes anyway (or at least I hoped), proposing on the beach with the help of your restaurant made this a dream-like experience for her and unforgettable for both of us. Anyway, with much sincerity, thank you very much for helping me create the best day of my life.

Respectfully,
"A very pleased customer"

GUESTS

Name		Message
Elise Allen Keith Gibson Baton Rouge LA	6/26	What a wonderful spot! Can't wait to return.
Pat & Stuart Kenney Woodstock, Ga	6/28	Perfect getaway! Thank you for the awesome service!
Kim & Karoline Leach The David Smith's		Best Panhandle Vacation of all Time. We'll never go anywhere else. Best of EVERYTHING GREAT STAFF! Th... As always, the best time, the best se... and the best people.
Matt & Jen Sleppy		Great stay, Great people, Great Eve... Great food, Great service, Great room...
Barbie Perkins-Cooper Mt. Pleasant, SC 29464		Absolutely a... hospitality ... Beautiful! Very Impre...
Matthew & Amanda Miklos Sacramento, CA		
John & Teresa Green Laurel Hill Fl		Beautif... wow... Se...
Matt & Kathleen Bade Grand Blanc, Mi		

Another Happy Day at Henderson Park Inn

During the summer months, with our suites nearly full, a young newlywed couple checked in to spend their honeymoon with us. As they were frolicking in the waist deep water, the groom's wedding ring slipped off his finger. When he realized it was not there, he started his frantic search. The bride was very upset and hurt, which made it of even more importance (if that could be possible). As more and more of our guests realized what was happening, they all proceeded to enter in the nearly impossible task of finding a needle in a haystack. There must have been fifteen guests out there wading in the surf. After a couple of hours of this and many tears and much frustration, everyone finally gave up. A local who had walked by and helped recommended a guy in the area who had a metal machine. This machine would work in water. After a couple more hours and the sun starting to set, the ring was unbelievably found. The groom was happy, the bride was happy, and everyone toasted to a job well done at our happy hour as the red-filled sky went down below the horizon. Another happy day at Henderson Park Inn. Thanks to all of our guests who were here that day to help out someone in need!

Jamee A Gaddis

Exceptional Guests

Sun-Dried Tomato Bruschetta

SERVING SIZE: 16

16 slices Italian bread
3 tablespoons Herb & Garlic Flavor Chef's Grill Plus® Instant Marinade
^{1}/$_2$ cup feta cheese – crumbled
^{1}/$_2$ cup oven-dried tomato – chopped
^{1}/$_4$ cup basil – chopped
1 recipe Garlic Aïoli (page 75)

Preheat a grill surface. Brush the bread lightly with the Chef's Grill Plus®.

Place the bread on the grill surface and brown well on both sides.

Top the grilled bread slices with the feta, tomato and basil. Drizzle the aïoli on top.

Coconut Shrimp with Jalapeno Dipping Sauce

Serving Size: 6

JALAPENO DIPPING SAUCE

- 1/2 cup chicken stock
- 1/2 each jalapeno – chopped
- 2 tablespoons rice vinegar
- 1 tablespoon oyster sauce
- 1 teaspoon sugar
- 1 teaspoon garlic – chopped

SHRIMP

- 1 teaspoon pickled ginger – chopped
- 1/2 cup all-purpose flour
- 1 cup shredded coconut
- 2 egg yolks
- 3/4 cup milk
- 2 egg whites
- 18 jumbo shrimp – peeled and deveined

For the sauce: Blend all the ingredients together and let stand for three hours.

For the shrimp: Preheat oil for frying to 350 degrees.

Blend the flour and coconut; gradually stir in the egg yolks and milk.

In a separate bowl beat the egg whites until stiff and fold into the batter.

Dip shrimp into batter and fry immediately; drain. Serve with the prepared sauce.

Crispy Shrimp Crostini with Marinara Sauce

Serving Size: 12

1 loaf French bread – sliced 1/4 inch thick
1/4 cup olive oil
1/4 recipe marinara sauce page 42
Flavors of the Gulf Coast
2 tablespoons Original Flavor
Chef's Grill Plus® Instant Marinade
1 egg

1/4 cup milk
36 (26- to 30-count) shrimp –
peeled and deveined
2 cups panko
1/2 cup canola oil
1/4 cup sour cream or mascarpone cheese
1/4 cup basil leaves – chopped fine

Preheat an oven to 375 degrees.

Toss the French bread in the olive oil and bake in the oven until golden brown.

Heat the marinara sauce and keep warm.

In a small bowl, whisk the Chef's Grill Plus®, egg and milk together.

Place the shrimp in the milk mixture and then the panko to coat.

Heat the canola oil in two large sauté pans and panfry the shrimp until golden brown.

Place one shrimp on top of a crouton, top with a teaspoon of marinara, 1/2 teaspoon of sour cream and garnish with the basil.

Fried Plantains

SERVING SIZE: 4

3 cups canola oil
to taste salt
3 plantains (or very ripe bananas) – see note

With adult supervision, heat oil to 350 degrees in a fry pan or electric fryer.

Put a little salt on plantains and fry until done.

NOTE: The thin lengthwise-sliced plantains will be a deep yellow and should be crisp. The thicker rounds will be brownish and crisp on the outside. The inside of the rounds should not be crisp. Store in paper bags.

She-Crab Soup

Serving Size: 8

1/2 stick unsalted butter	2 teaspoons cayenne pepper
1/4 cup all-purpose flour	2 tablespoons Worcestershire sauce
1 cup yellow onion – minced	2 pounds special white crab meat –
1 tablespoon garlic – chopped	picked clean
to taste kosher salt	1/2 cup dry sherry
to taste white pepper	pinch of lemon zest
2 teaspoons mace	1/2 cup crab roe, or 2 hard-boiled
3 cups milk	egg yolks coarsely chopped
2 cups heavy cream	1 tablespoon parsley – finely chopped

In a top of a double boiler melt the butter completely and slowly incorporate the flour. Cook the mixture for 3 to 5 minutes to create a roux. Stir in the onion and garlic. Season with salt, white pepper and mace.

Cook the mixture for 5 minutes; whisk in the milk, heavy cream, cayenne and Worcestershire. Bring the liquid to a boil and reduce to a simmer.

Simmer the soup for 15 minutes. Stir in the crab and continue simmering for 10 to 15 minutes, then check seasoning again.

To serve, ladle the soup into bowls, drizzle with the sherry and garnish with the lemon zest, crab roe and parsley.

SERVING IDEA: In some areas of the country blue crab and crab roe may not be available, so select the best and freshest crab product from your region as a substitute. Also if crab roe is difficult, hard-boiled egg yolks coarsely chopped work well.

Lobster Bisque

Serving Size: 10

3	tablespoons olive oil	1/2	cup sherry
3	each (1 1/2- to 2-pound) lobster shells and bodies reserved from cooking – chopped	1	sprig whole thyme
		1	teaspoon black pepper – crushed
1	large yellow onion – coarsely chopped	1	each bay leaf
2	each rib celery – coarsely chopped	1/2	cup tomato paste
2	each carrots – coarsely chopped		blonde roux
2	cloves garlic – crushed		heavy cream
1/4	cup brandy		to taste kosher salt
1	cup white wine		to taste white pepper

Heat the oil in a braising pan. Add the lobster shells and vegetables and sauté until slightly browned.

Deglaze with the brandy and transfer all into a 12-quart pot.

Add the wine, sherry, herbs, tomato paste and 1 1/2 gallons of warm water.

Bring to a rolling boil and then reduce to a low boil for 2 hours, skimming constantly.

Remove the stock from the heat and strain through a fine strainer, cool and refrigerate or use for cooking.

Bring the stock to a boil. Add the blonde roux and cream, then low boil for 20 minutes skimming occasionally.

Add additional tomato paste if needed and season to taste.

Serve immediately or cool and refrigerate and best served one day old and reheated to a boil.

NOTE: For a Thai version substitute coconut milk for the cream, cut the tomato paste by half and season to taste with red curry paste. Finish with button mushrooms and a crushed kaffir lime leaf and garnish with chopped cilantro.

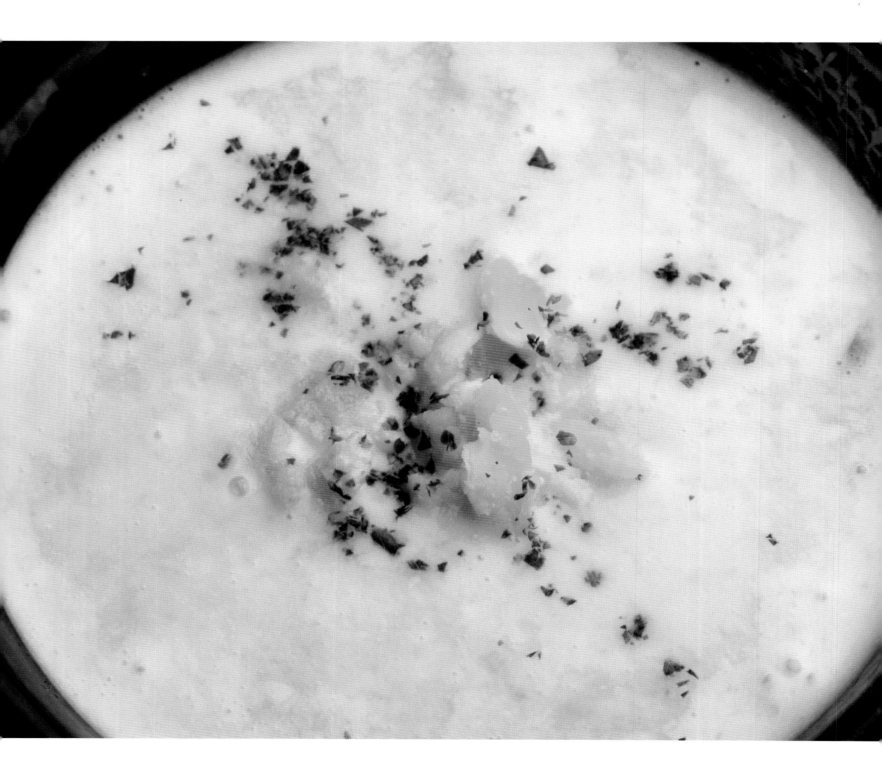

Cheddar, Pancetta and Leek Soup

Serving Size: 8

1 stick butter	3 cups chicken stock
4 leeks – white only, split and diced	2 cups cream
2 celery stalks – diced small	$1/2$ pound Cheddar cheese – grated
2 carrots – peeled and diced small	2 teaspoons Crystal hot sauce
2 garlic cloves – minced	$1/2$ cup pancetta – fried crispy
to taste salt	and chopped
to taste pepper	2 tablespoons green onions – chopped
3 tablespoons flour	

In a heavy-bottomed soup pot, melt the butter and sauté the vegetables for 5 minutes on medium heat.

Add the garlic and season with salt and pepper. Add the flour and blend well.

Stir in the chicken stock, cream and cheese. Bring the liquid to a boil and reduce to simmer for 30 minutes.

Remove from the heat and purée with a stick blender.

Add the hot sauce and pancetta and return to a boil.

Serve garnished with green onions and bread.

SERVING IDEAS: Great with some crispy warm bread.

Roasted Tomato Soup

Serving Size: 4

4	each tomatoes – tops removed	3	tablespoons tomato paste
1/2	each red onion – quartered	1	cup heavy cream
5	cloves garlic	2	tablespoons fresh basil – chopped
3	tablespoons olive oil	to taste salt	
2	ounces bacon – chopped	to taste pepper	
4	cups chicken stock		

Coat tomatoes, onions and garlic with olive oil and place in 400-degree oven until brown.

Render bacon in heavy-bottomed sauce pot.

Add roasted tomatoes, onion and garlic; sauté for 5 minutes.

Add chicken stock and simmer covered for 15 minutes.

Purée with hand blender or in a blender, adding the tomato paste.

Return to the pan and simmer another 10 minutes.

Add cream and basil and season to taste.

Serve hot or cold.

Starlit Dinners

Bay Shrimp Gumbo

Spicy Pomodoro Shrimp

Garlic and Herb Bronzed
Hawaiian Sea Bass

Calabash Fish Fry

Chicken Breast Stuffed with
Fontina Cheese and Spinach

Southern Fried Chicken

Chicken and Dumplings

Duck Breast or Pork Tenderloin Moo Yang

Howell Fried Turkey Strips

Pork Grillades

Oven-Roasted Pork Loin

Perfect Baby Back Ribs

Tomato Stewed Cabbage with Caramelized Onion

Sautéed Baby Carrots and Green Beans

Collard Greens

Fried Okra

Fried Okra Salad

Fresh Black-Eyed Pea, Red Onion and Apple Salsa

Potato, Napa Cabbage, Applewood Bacon,
Mushroom and Leek Casserole

Penne with Roasted Red Pepper Sauce

Grill Baked Sweet Potato with Brown Sugar

Eggplant Medallions with Crab Meat

Aunt Jacque's Cheese Grits

Exceptional Taste

Bay Shrimp Gumbo

Serving Size: 8

1/2 stick unsalted butter
1 large yellow onion – diced fine
2 stalks celery – diced fine
1 teaspoon garlic – chopped
1/4 cup all-purpose flour
2 cans Rotel tomatoes – chopped fine with juice
1 can tomato purée
4 cups water

2 bay leaves
2 cups baby shrimp – peeled
1 cup fish trimmings – chopped
1 teaspoon Zatarain's liquid crab boil
to taste Tabasco sauce
2 tablespoons Tony Chachere's Creole Original – or to taste
3 tablespoons Worcestershire sauce
5 cups rice – cooked

In a soup pot, melt the butter and sauté the onion, celery and garlic for 5 minutes. Add the flour and blend in well. Add the tomatoes and purée and bring to a boil.

Add the water and bay leaves; bring to a boil for 20 minutes.

Add the shrimp and fish and boil until cooked through.

Season with crab boil, Tabasco, Tony's and Worcestershire.

Serve with cooked rice.

Spicy Pomodoro Shrimp

Serving Size: 4

1/2   cup white wine
12   each jumbo gulf shrimp – peeled and deveined
1   tablespoon garlic – chopped
1   cup Italian plum tomato – chopped
to taste crushed red pepper
2   tablespoons basil – chopped
to taste salt

In a sauce pot, bring the wine to a boil.

Add the remaining ingredients and cook shrimp to desired doneness; remove the shrimp and set aside.

Reduce the sauce to the desired thickness and season to taste.

Garnish as desired.

Garlic and Herb Bronzed Hawaiian Sea Bass

Serving Size: 4

4   each (6-ounce) sea bass fillets
4   tablespoons Herb & Garlic Flavor
Chef's Grill Plus® Instant Marinade

Preheat an oven to 400 degrees and a cast-iron skillet till very hot.

Brush the sea bass on one side with the Chef's Grill Plus®.

Place brushed side down in the skillet. Paint the other side and flip all the fillets once the first fillet that was placed in the skillet browns.

Place in the oven and bake until desired temperature.

Serve immediately.

Calabash Fish Fry

Serving Size: 4

1/2 cup horseradish
1/2 cup sour cream
to taste kosher salt
1/4 cup all-purpose flour
2 eggs
2/3 cup cornmeal

1 cup seasoned bread crumbs
2 pounds fresh fish fillets – cut into thin pieces
1 cup cooking oil
2 lemons – cut into quarters for garnish

Blend the horseradish and sour cream and season to taste with salt; set aside.

In a shallow large casserole dish, place the flour. In a mixing bowl with a whisk beat the eggs with 2 teaspoons of water. In another casserole dish combine the cornmeal and bread crumbs.

Dip the fish pieces in the flour, then into the egg mixture, then in the cornmeal mixture until coated.

In a large cast-iron skillet, bring cooking oil to 350 degrees for frying. Fry the fish for about 5 minutes or until brown, crispy and flaky.

Drain on paper towels and serve with lemon and horseradish sauce.

Chicken Breast Stuffed with Fontina Cheese and Spinach

Serving Size: 4

4 skinless boneless chicken breasts – pounded	to taste white pepper
1 cup fontina cheese – grated	1/4 cup Original Flavor Chef's Grill Plus® Instant Marinade
1 cup fresh spinach – wilted	1/2 cup milk
12 toothpicks	1 cup white flour
to taste salt	1/4 cup melted butter

Preheat an oven to 400 degrees.

Lay the pounded chicken breasts flat on a work surface smooth side down.

Distribute the cheese and spinach equally among the 4 breasts.

Roll up the chicken and secure with toothpicks; season with the salt and white pepper.

Blend the Chef's Grill Plus® and milk together in a small mixing bowl.

Dredge the chicken rolls through the flour, then the milk mixture and back into the flour.

Place the butter in a baking dish; roll the chicken in the butter and bake for 15 minutes or until cooked through.

Let rest 5 minutes, slice and serve.

Southern Fried Chicken

Serving Size: 4

3	each whole eggs	2	teaspoons ground black pepper
1/3	cup hot water	1	each whole chicken – cut into
to taste	Crystal hot sauce		8 pieces
1/2	gallon canola oil	to taste	kosher salt
3	cups self-rising flour	to taste	granulated garlic

In a medium-size bowl, beat the eggs with the water. Add hot sauce to taste—don't be shy!

Preheat the oil in a heavy-bottomed pot no more than half full to 350 degrees.

In another bowl combine the flour and pepper. Season the chicken pieces generously with equal parts of salt and granulated garlic. Dredge the chicken in the egg and then coat well with the flour mixture.

Fry the chicken in the oil until brown and crisp. Dark meat takes about 15 minutes and the white meat takes about 10 minutes.

CHICKEN AND DUMPLINGS

SERVING SIZE: 12

1/3	cup shortening	1	large box chicken broth
1	cup hot water	1	can cream of chicken soup
1	large egg	1	can cream of mushroom soup
1	teaspoon salt		to taste kosher salt
3	cups flour		to taste white pepper
1	whole chicken		

Dissolve shortening in hot water. Let cool until warm. Mix in egg and salt.

Gradually add in flour; it will be sticky and gooey.

Roll out dough thin on a floured work surface. Allow to rest for 15 minutes and then cut into two-inch-wide strips.

Boil chicken in a large pot, covering the chicken with broth and water. When chicken is done, debone and set meat aside; discard skin and bones.

Add the two cans soup to broth and bring to a boil.

Drop dumplings into boiling broth and allow dumplings to develop a little texture, about 10 minutes, then add chicken.

Reduce heat and simmer 20 to 25 minutes.

Place lid on pot and remove from heat. Allow to sit 20 minutes; check seasonings, then serve.

Duck Breast or Pork Tenderloin Moo Yang

Serving Size: 4

2 tablespoons oyster sauce
1/4 cup sugar
3 tablespoons dark soy
3 tablespoons soy sauce
3 tablespoons honey
3 tablespoons sriracha
1 tablespoon rice vinegar

2 teaspoons garlic – chopped
4 each Maple Leaf Farms duck breasts (pounded and skin cut diagonally 1 inch apart), or pork tenderloins (cut thinly on a bias)
2 sprigs cilantro – chopped

Blend all the ingredients, except duck breast and cilantro. Mix well and place in a sealable plastic bag or marinating vessel with the duck breast or sliced pork for a minimum of one hour or refrigerate overnight.

Preheat a grill surface on high. Grill duck breast or pork until desired temperature. Serve sliced and garnished with fresh chopped cilantro.

Howell Fried Turkey Strips

Serving size: 2

6 wild turkey breast strips, cut 3/4 inch thick and 1 inch wide
Several cloves of garlic, peeled, cut in half and slightly crushed
3 tablespoons each ground black pepper and salt – mixed together

Milk
Chef's Grill Plus® Instant Marinade
All-purpose flour
3 teaspoons butter
3 tablespoons olive oil

Score the breast strips all over with a sharp knife or perforate with a fork. Rub each strip on both sides with a cut garlic clove. Shake the ground black pepper and salt mixture on both sides of the strips.

Prepare a milk wash by mixing 3 parts milk to 1 part Chef's Grill Plus®.

Dip the strips in the milk wash. Place in a sealable plastic bag with flour and shake until fully coated.

Melt the butter with the olive oil in a large cast-iron skillet. When the mixture of oil and butter is hot, add the turkey strips. Fry them on each side, about 3 minutes in all.

Serve hot and enjoy.

NOTE: *"Plus it up" with Chef's Grill Plus® Instant Marinade.*

Pork Grillades

Serving Size: 4

1 1/2   pounds pork cheeks or butt – cut into 1-inch cubes
2   tablespoons flour
1   each yellow onion – diced
1   teaspoon garlic – chopped
1   cup peeled tomatoes with juice – chopped
1   teaspoon cayenne pepper
1   each bell pepper – diced
1   sprig parsley – chopped
1   cup hot water
2   teaspoons salt
1   cup mushrooms – sliced

In a heavy-bottomed pot, brown the pork well; remove from the pot, reserving the drippings.

Brown the flour in the drippings; return the pork and add the remaining ingredients. Simmer for up to 2 hours or until the meat is tender.

Oven-Roasted Pork Loin

Serving Size: 8

1   (3- to 4-pound) pork loin
1   container favorite flavor Chef's Grill Plus® Instant Marinade

Preheat an oven to 425 degrees.

Brush the pork loin generously with Chef's Grill Plus® and place on a rack in a roasting pan.

Cook to an internal temperature of 130 degrees; let rest 10 minutes. Slice thinly and serve.

Perfect Baby Back Ribs

Serves 6

3 slabs of baby back ribs
Mesquite Flavor Chef's Grill Plus®
1 large bottle of Bull's-Eye Original Barbecue Sauce

Day before serving:
Preheat an oven to 225 degrees. Remove ribs from package and pat dry. Season with Chef's Grill Plus®. Place ribs in a roasting pan so they are standing upright leaning on each other. Pour 1/2 of the barbecue sauce on top. Cover with plastic wrap and then foil. Place in oven and cook for 5 hours. Let cool in the refrigerator overnight.

Day of serving:
Preheat grill to high. Remove ribs from roasting pan and brush with the remainder of the barbecue sauce. Reheat on the grill 4 to 5 minutes on each side. Serve immediately.

Tomato Stewed Cabbage with Caramelized Onion

Serving Size: 6

3 tablespoons salad oil
1 head savoy cabbage – coarsely chopped
2 each vine-ripe tomatoes – diced
1 tablespoon Worcestershire sauce

3 tablespoons sugar
to taste kosher salt
to taste black pepper
to taste Crystal hot sauce
1 each yellow onion – caramelized

Heat the oil in a large pot or braising pan.

Add the cabbage and tomatoes and cook over medium heat for 10 minutes, stirring often.

Add the Worcestershire and sugar and continue for 10 more minutes on medium to high heat; reduce to simmer.

After simmering for 20 minutes, season to taste. Toss in caramelized onion; keep warm or serve immediately.

NOTE: To caramelize an onion, slice thin and sauté over medium heat in a large sauté pan with 2 tablespoons of butter until very brown; season to taste.

Sautéed Baby Carrots and Green Beans

Serving Size: 4

2 tablespoons unsalted butter – melted
16 each baby carrots – peeled and blanched
1/4 pound haricots verts (baby green beans) – snapped and blanched
to taste kosher salt
to taste fresh ground black pepper

In a large sauté pan, heat the butter; add the carrots and beans. Sauté on medium heat to desired doneness and then season to taste.

Serve immediately.

COLLARD GREENS

SERVING SIZE: 8

3 quarts water
1/2 pound pork hocks – smoked
1 teaspoon kosher salt
1 teaspoon ground black pepper
3 teaspoons fresh garlic
2 tablespoons Crystal hot sauce
1 large bag cleaned collards
2 tablespoons butter

Bring the water to a boil in a large pot and add the smoked pork, seasonings and hot sauce.

Chop the collards into large dice and put them in the boiling water mixture. Reduce to medium heat and cook at least 1 hour.

Add the butter, adjust seasonings and serve.

Henderson Beach State Park—
An Unforgettable Creation

Neighboring Henderson Park Inn to the West, Henderson Beach State Park's 6,000 feet of unspoiled Emerald Beach, dunes, and nature preserve is forever protected and provides the most beautiful views in the State of Florida.

Named for its previous owner, Bernie Henderson, the Park was purchased in 1983 and opened to the public in 1991. The Park has a unique and interesting history.

Originally owned by the Federal Government, the Park and much of the surrounding land, had virgin timber that was used for building wooden sailing ships. Prior to 1928, the Navy ceased the construction of wooden sailing vessels and elected to sell the property preserved for this use, some 36,000 acres, a portion of which being what is now Henderson Beach State Park. At this time, there were approximately twenty-five fishing families living in homes along the Gulf Coast in this area, and the Department of Navy gave each family the opportunity to buy the land where their homes were constructed. The price was $50 per acre (now it's a bargain at tens of thousands a foot), and many of the families purchased their homestead, paying through a federal program established to make it fair for them.

Exceptional Place

J.R. Moody, a turpentine business man from Vernon, Florida, bought the rest of the 36,000 acres for around $36,000. He was strictly interested in the timber, and, since he wasn't interested in the dazzling white sand of the beach, he sold roughly six miles of the beachfront to Mr. Broughton Wilkerson for some $25,000. To Mr. Moody this land was pure folly, since there was nothing in that strip but sugar-white sand and not enough timber to build a campfire.

A year later, Mr. Brighton sold half the property (three miles) to the Henderson family, represented by Bernie Henderson. After another year, he sold Mr. Henderson the other three miles. Although not validated, it is believed that upwards of $75,000 changed hands on that shifting of title.

Inset photo: View of Henderson Beach State Park from 3rd floor balcony at Henderson Park Inn

In 1983, after several years of hard work maneuvering through the State Funding system by Mr. Davage (Buddy) Runnels, the State of Florida purchased 6,000 feet of the Henderson's six miles and created the Henderson Beach State Park. In 1991 the Park was opened to the public, and today the Henderson Park Inn abuts the Eastern property boundary of the Park, overlooking this unforgettable creation.

Some time ago, Billy Dunavant, Chairman of the Board, and William (Bill) Hagerman, Vice President of Dunavant Enterprises, saw the vast potential of a vision which is now in the advanced planning stage: Creating a resort to preserve a forever view of the world's most beautiful beach and the timeless serenity of Henderson Beach State Park.

Fried Okra

Serving Size: 6

2/3 cup white flour	4 cups canola oil
1/3 cup cornmeal	1 1/2 bags frozen cut okra
1 tablespoon kosher salt	3/4 cup buttermilk
1 tablespoon black pepper	

Blend the flours and seasonings.

Preheat the oil to 350 degrees and prepare a drain board.

Dip the okra in the buttermilk and shake off excess. Dip into the flour mixture and shake off excess and repeat until all the okra is battered.

Gently drop the okra into the oil and with a screen or slotted spoon, stir around and separate.

Fry until golden brown and crispy; drain and serve immediately.

Fried Okra Salad

Serving Size: 6

1/4 cup white vinegar
1/3 cup canola oil
1/4 cup sugar
2 large tomatoes – seeded and chopped
1/2 gold bell pepper – diced
6 slices bacon – fried crisp and chopped
1 batch Fried Okra – (see page 130)
to taste kosher salt
to taste fresh ground black pepper

In a small saucepan, combine the vinegar, oil and sugar and heat until the sugar melts. Set aside.

Toss the tomatoes with the pepper and bacon and add the fried okra.

Toss with the desired amount of dressing and season to taste.

Fresh Black-Eyed Pea, Red Onion and Apple Salsa

Serving Size: 4

2 cups chicken stock
pinch of salt
1 cup fresh black-eyed peas – shucked
1/2 red onion – diced fine
1/2 cup apple cider
1 Granny Smith apple – diced fine

1/2 cup apple sauce
1/2 teaspoon chipotle chile canned in adobo – minced
2 tablespoons unsalted butter – melted
to taste salt

In a sauce pot, bring the stock and pinch of salt to a boil; add the peas and cook for 15 minutes or until tender.

In a sauté pan, cook the remaining ingredients in the butter for 5 minutes. Remove from the heat and set aside.

Drain the peas well, toss with the sautéed mixture and season to taste. Serve warm or cold.

Potato, Napa Cabbage, Applewood Bacon, Mushroom and Leek Casserole

Serving Size: 6

1/2 cup applewood bacon – diced small	to taste salt
2 cups leeks – julienned	to taste black pepper
1 teaspoon garlic – chopped	3 each medium Idaho potatoes –
3 cups napa cabbage – julienned	peeled, washed and very thinly sliced
2 cups sautéed assorted sliced mushrooms	1/2 stick butter – melted

Preheat an oven to 375 degrees.

Heat a large sauté pan and add the bacon. Once the fat starts rendering out, add the leeks, garlic and napa cabbage. Sauté for 3 minutes, then add the mushrooms. Season this mixture to taste; set aside.

Place this mixture on a 9- × 12-inch baking pan and layer the potatoes evenly to cover the mixture completely. Drizzle butter over the potatoes. Season again to taste.

Place in the oven until the potatoes brown well; remove and let cool at room temperature.

With a ring cutter, cut 2 1/2-inch circles. Chop up the excess and divide equally among half the rings. Top the covered rings with the uncovered ones and reheat at 375 degrees; serve immediately.

Penne with Roasted Red Pepper Sauce

SERVING SIZE: 4

2 tablespoons olive oil
4 each garlic cloves – minced
2 cups roasted red sweet peppers
1 cup heavy cream
1/2 pound penne rigate – cooked, chilled and tossed in oil

to taste kosher salt
to taste fresh ground black pepper
1/2 each juice of a lemon
1/4 cup fresh basil – chopped
to taste reggiano parmesan – grated

In a saucepan, heat the oil. Add the garlic and cook, stirring until light brown. Add peppers and cook 7 minutes, stirring occasionally.

Blend with a hand mixer until puréed.

Add the cream and bring to a simmer. Add the pasta to heat.

Season to taste. Add lemon juice and serve garnished with the basil and cheese.

Grill Baked Sweet Potato with Brown Sugar

Serving Size: 4

2 each large sweet potato – split
2 tablespoons unsalted butter
2 tablespoons brown sugar
to taste salt
to taste fresh ground black pepper

Preheat a grill surface on high.

Place the potatoes skin side down on a large piece of heavy-duty foil.

Divide the butter and sugar equally among the potatoes and season to taste.

Wrap tightly in the foil and place skin side down on the grill surface, covered if possible, for at least 30 minutes or until a toothpick or fork tests soft.

Remove and serve immediately.

EGGPLANT MEDALLIONS WITH CRAB MEAT

SERVING SIZE: 2 to 4

EGGPLANT
Canola oil for frying
1/2 cup milk
1/4 cup Original Flavor Chef's Grill Plus®
Instant Marinade
1 peeled and sliced eggplant
2 cups corn flour
12 (3-inch) chive stems

SAUTÉED LUMP CRAB MEAT
1/4 stick butter
1/2 pound jumbo lump crab meat
1 chopped green onion
2 teaspoons lemon juice
to taste salt
to taste black pepper

For preparing the eggplant, preheat oil to 350 degrees in a deep fryer or electric skillet. Mix the milk and Chef's Grill Plus® in a bowl. Dip the eggplant into the milk mixture and coat with corn flour. Fry till golden brown; drain on paper towels.

For preparing the lump crab meat, melt butter in a sauté pan on low-medium heat. Mix in the crab meat and stir gently until butter has coated entire surface of meat, approximately 1 to 2 minutes. Add additional ingredients and simmer until warmed through.

For the assembly, place the eggplant on the center of the plates and top each with prepared crab meat. Drizzle with ranch dressing and garnish with chives.

Bill Hagerman says, "For the healthy eater, get two orders and you can feel good that you didn't eat three."

Aunt Jacque's Cheese Grits

Serving Size: 12

5½ cups water
1 cup quick stone-ground grits
3 teaspoons Lawry's seasoned salt
1 stick butter

1 pound Velveeta cheese
3 eggs
½ cup water

Preheat an oven to 350 degrees.

Take a large glass Pyrex dish and bring the 5½ cups of water to boil in a microwave for 5 minutes.

Add the grits and seasoned salt and microwave on high 10 minutes.

Add the butter and cheese and microwave on high 5 minutes.

Mix the eggs and ½ cup of water together, then slowly add a little grits to this mixture; to be sure not to cook the eggs as you are adding together, do this slowly.

Spray a 9- × 13-inch glass Pyrex dish with nonstick spray.

Bake 1 hour at 350 degrees.

Let it set for 15 to 20 minutes and it will firm up.

Serve immediately.

NOTE: May add garlic powder for additional flavor.

Sweet Evenings

Peaches au Flan or Brûlée

Painkiller Cake

Almond Pound Cake

Italian Doughnuts

Charlotte Hickox's
Homemade Grape-Nut Ice Cream

Pecan Pie

Pumpkin Pie

White and Dark Chocolate–Covered
Applewood Bacon

Exceptional Taste

Peaches au Flan or Brûlée

Serving Size: 6

2¹/₂ cups heavy cream
¹/₃ cup sugar
2 each egg yolks
1 each whole egg
1 tablespoon vanilla extract

3 each fresh peaches – peeled, split and seed removed

BRÛLÉE TOPPING
1 tablespoon brown sugar
4 tablespoons granulated sugar

Preheat an oven to 325 degrees.

Heat the cream with the sugar until melted; do not boil. Let stand at room temperature for 10 minutes.

Whisk the eggs with the vanilla and incorporate into the cream mixture.

Place the peaches round side up in individual shallow ramekins or brûlée dishes. Pour the cream mixture until the peach shows just like an egg sunny side up.

Repeat this step 5 more times and place the ramekins in a deep roasting pan; add enough water to cover halfway up the outside of the ramekin.

Place in the oven for 20 to 25 minutes or until the custard is firm to the touch. Remove and let cool to room temperature or refrigerate for up to 2 days.

Combine the two sugars for the brûlée topping and spread over the top of each dessert. Using a propane torch, brown and crisp the sugar; do not burn. Serve immediately.

Painkiller Cake

Serving Size: 8

1 package yellow cake mix with pudding in it

1 small package Jello Instant White Chocolate Pudding

5 eggs

1/2 cup orange juice

3/4 cup Pusser's Rum

1/2 cup Coco Lopez

1 stick butter

2 cups sugar

1/2 cup pineapple juice

1/2 cup orange juice

1 cup Pusser's Rum

to taste fresh nutmeg – grated

Preheat an oven to 350 degrees.

Blend the cake mix, pudding mix, eggs, 1/2 cup orange juice, 3/4 cup Pusser's Rum and Coco Lopez well in a mixer.

Pour into a buttered nonstick bundt pan.

Bake for 45 minutes and test with a toothpick at 40 minutes, to be sure to not overcook.

Remove and set out to cool for 5 minutes; flip the cake out of the pan onto a server.

While the cake is baking, make the glaze by bringing the butter, sugar and remaining juices to a slow boil for 3 minutes.

Add 1 cup rum and the nutmeg and simmer for an additional 5 minutes or until glaze is thick. (On gas cooktops, be aware that the rum may ignite when added—use caution.)

Drizzle the glaze over the cake. Serve warm or at room temperature.

Almond Pound Cake

Serving Size: 8

12 tablespoons unsalted butter – room temperature and chopped	1/3 cup canola oil
1 1/2 cups sugar	10 each eggs
24 ounces almond paste	1 cup all-purpose flour
4 each lemons – zest only	2 teaspoons baking powder
	6 tablespoons Triple Sec

Preheat an oven to 325 degrees.

Cream the butter and sugar together until smooth.

Add almond paste in small chunks; add the zest and continue to cream.

Add the oil and beat until all is incorporated. Add the eggs one at a time, blending completely after each addition.

Mix in the flour and baking powder and blend completely.

Place in a greased loaf pan and bake for an hour, checking doneness with a wooden skewer.

Remove and brush with Triple Sec. Cool and serve.

Italian Doughnuts

Serving Size: 8

1	batch sausage bread dough	1/4	cup cinnamon
3/4	cup granulated sugar	2	gallons canola oil

After the dough has risen, tear into 2-ounce pieces and let rise again for 30 minutes.

Blend the sugar and cinnamon together. Set aside.

Preheat the oil to 345 degrees.

Have a sheet pan lined with paper towels ready.

Carefully drop the dough pieces into the oil 4 to 5 at a time, rolling occasionally with a slotted spoon.

Fry until golden brown and firm. Place on the paper towels and let drain. Dust with the sugar mixture.

Serve immediately.

NOTE: *May be served with fresh berry sauce, warm chocolate sauce, cream, or jelly.*

Future Expectations

The beachfront Henderson Park Inn and the properties to the north of the Inn were purchased in 2005 by an affiliate of Dunavant Enterprises, Inc. in Memphis, Tennessee. Because of its location next to the nature preserves of the Henderson Beach State Park, the unique sugar-white sand along the Inn and the Park properties, the spectacular sunsets, and the close proximity to private and public golf, shopping, and the airport, the land is scheduled to be a Dunavant Signature Property. Joining such prestigious Dunavant projects as the World Golf Village in St. Augustine, Florida, home of the World Golf Hall of Fame, PGA Broadcasting Headquarters, and two co-signature world-class golf courses (the King & Bear and the Slammer & Squire), the Henderson Park Inn property will become the Henderson Beach Resort.

The Resort, when finished, will a be pedestrian-focused, town center–style themed community encompassing a world-class resort hotel with a signature restaurant, spa, meeting facilities, shops, swimming pools, grass malls and parks, an active esplanade, access to a private golf course, and many other features. Accompanying the Resort hotel will be over three-hundred private luxury residences having varying views of the Gulf, the town center, the malls and parks, and the Henderson Beach State Park.

Exceptional Resort

Although the current quaint New England-style Henderson Park Inn Bed-and-Breakfast will remain far into the first phases of the Resort project, the wooden structure currently comprising the Inn and its close proximity to the waves of the Gulf make it impossible for it to remain long term. However, the charm, grace, exceptional service, and friendly staff that guests currently experience at the Henderson Park Inn, along with the beachside verandas, spectacular sunsets, and mile of unspoiled beach, will be the cornerstones of the new Henderson Beach Resort.

HENDERSON BEACH RESORT

Charlotte Hickox's Homemade Grape-Nut Ice Cream

SERVING SIZE: 15 to 20

2	cups milk	4	cups (1 quart) whipping cream
3	eggs	2	cups Grape-Nuts cereal
1	cup sugar	1	teaspoon vanilla extract
4	cups (1 quart) half-and-half		

Combine the milk, eggs and sugar in a large saucepan and heat over low to medium heat until thickened. Stir in the half-and-half and cream until well combined.

Remove from the heat and stir in the cereal and vanilla.

Pour into an ice cream freezer container and freeze using the manufacturer's directions.

Pecan Pie

Serving Size: 6

3   large eggs, beaten
1   cup sugar
1   cup light or dark corn syrup
3   tablespoons melted butter
1   teaspoon vanilla
1½   cups pecan halves
1   unbaked 9-inch pie shell

Mix all ingredients.

Add pecans last.

Pour into unbaked pie shell.

Bake at 350 degrees for 50 to 55 minutes.

Pumpkin Pie

Serving Size: 6

1 cup granulated sugar	1/4 cup corn syrup
1 3/4 cups light brown sugar	1 pound pumpkin
pinch of salt	1 1/2 cups milk
1 teaspoon cinnamon, ground	2 each eggs, beaten
1/2 teaspoon of nutmeg, ground	1 unbaked (9-inch) pie shell
2 tablespoons bread flour	

Mix the sugars, salt and spices.

Stir in flour.

Add the syrup, pumpkin and milk. Let rest overnight.

Blend in eggs.

Spread in unbaked pie shell.

Bake at 400 degrees for 45 minutes or until filling is set but still soft.

White and Dark Chocolate–Covered Applewood Bacon

SERVING SIZE: 6

1 cup white covering chocolate
1 cup dark covering chocolate
12 each applewood bacon strips – cooked crisp and chilled

Melt each chocolate on a low-heat double boiler until completely melted.

Place the bacon strips on wax paper.

With a spoon, cover half the bacon strip with the white chocolate; do the opposite end with the dark chocolate, overlapping slightly. Let cool and serve.

Like Father, Like Son...

"Nothing was forgotten in the planning of the Inn, and the day it opened (which ironically was Tax Day—April 15th), is a day that is imprinted in my mind forever. There may be many more bed-and-breakfasts built, but none with as much heart, history, and passion put into it as the Henderson Park Inn," says Jim. Having spent many years as the CEO for Bill and Steve Abbott, Jim Olin recalls his time at Henderson Park Inn fondly.

Amazingly enough, when the Inn reopened for business in 2006, Olin's oldest son Ryan was named as the new Innkeeper and still keeps daily watch on the Inn today. Times have changed, operation methods are a little different, but a heart for making the Inn a special place for every guest was passed from father to son, and Ryan continues the tradition of guest care that his father instilled.

McCabe Olin, Ryan's one-year-old son, has already started making friends at the Inn, getting ready for his reign of succession to come.

Exceptional Future

Dunavant Enterprises

Dunavant Enterprises, Inc., was the largest privately owned cotton merchandiser in the world, handling in excess of six million bales of cotton per year, until the Dunavant family made the strategic decision to exit the cotton business in 2008 to focus on other sectors. Through four generations, the Dunavant family has been involved in the cotton industry, first as a cotton producer near Tunica, Mississippi, later as a pioneer of railroading, hauling cotton in the Mississippi Delta, and in recent times, as the owners and operators of one of the world's largest and most successful cotton merchandising firms. Dunavant helped set the pace for the entire cotton industry through its timing, flexibility, and strategic business integration in all of the industry's critical functions: information, buying and selling, ginning, warehousing, and trading. Dunavant's presence has made an impact throughout the cotton trading world.

Building on his father Buck Dunavant's legacy, former CEO and current Chairman of the Board William B. (Billy) Dunavant Jr. was instrumental in creating a global market for cotton at a time when trading was only regional in scope. Under his leadership, the company adopted a far more aggressive and innovative business model, initiating "forward contracting" and recognizing early on the potential for U.S. cotton sales into export markets. The firm grew from a small scale Memphis trader into a cotton merchant handling all world growths, participating in the first sale of U.S. cotton to China in the early 1970s. Throughout the '80s, '90s and into the 2000s, the company expanded its operations into all regions where cotton is of economic importance through acquisition or construction of fixed assets in remote areas, including cotton gins and warehouses in the American Southwest, Australia, Central Asia, and Eastern Africa. Dunavant Enterprises grew to be a company ranked by Forbes 60th among best small companies in America, with 9 appearances on the Forbes 500 "Largest Private Companies" list.

Dunavant has been a finalist in the U.S. Secretary of State's Award for Corporate Excellence for its work in Africa toward HIV/Aids prevention and for its contribution to economic growth in Zambia. By creating a program in Mozambique for small farmers to improve their cotton yields, Dunavant Enterprises secured an award to the program of $8 million from the Bill and Melinda Gates Foundation. These projects contributed to the company's recognition as one of *Ethisphere Magazine's* "World's Most Ethical Companies," reflecting Billy Dunavant's lifetime of service impacting countless individuals.

Along the way, Mr. Dunavant's entrepreneurial spirit and sense of duty to his community has led to forays into a number of non-cotton related ventures. Dunavant has owned and operated companies engaged in aviation, software development, professional football and tennis, real estate development, offshore supply vessels, and logistics. Drawing on Dunavant's depth of experience in movement of cotton worldwide, the company created Centrix Logistics in 2009. Centrix is a federally licensed freight forwarder and full-service provider of a broad spectrum of logistics and consulting services based in Memphis, Tennessee.

Dunavant Gulf, LLC, is the current owner of The Henderson Park Inn and future developer of Destin's Henderson Beach Resort. For nearly thirty years Dunavant Enterprises has been involved in all types of land development and conservation projects, including the World Golf Village in St. Augustine, Florida, featuring The Slammer and the Squire (Snead and Sarazen) and The King and the Bear (Palmer and Nicklaus) cosignatory golf courses, the World Golf Hall of Fame, and the Neighborhoods of the World Golf Village. Mr. Dunavant also founded The Racquet Club of Memphis and brought world-class tennis to his hometown of Memphis with the U.S. Indoor tournament, now the St. Jude International Tennis Championship. Dunavant Development is also involved in many other industrial, commercial, and residential developments across the southeastern U.S. The acquisition of The Henderson Inn Park property and planned development of The Henderson Beach Resort reflect the company's strategy of selecting and participating in quality projects that are in keeping with the prestige and high standards of the Dunavant name.

HENDERSON BEACH RESORT

2700 Scenic Highway 98
Destin, Florida 32459